£1

EASY TO MAKE

NURSERY CRAFTS

EASY TO MAKE
NURSERY CRAFTS
AUDREY VINCENTE DEAN

ANAYA PUBLISHERS LTD LONDON

First published in Great Britain in 1994
by Anaya Publishers Ltd, Strode House,
44–50 Osnaburgh Street, London NW1 3ND

For Harry, of course.

Editor Eve Harlow
Design Millions Design
Photography Steve Tanner
Charts and illustrations Terry Evans

British Library in Publication Data

Vincente Dean, Audrey

Easy to make nursery crafts. – (Easy to make)
1. Nursery crafts. 2 Crafts
1. Title 11. Series
ISBN 1 85470 172 X

Typeset by Servis Filmsetting Ltd, Manchester, UK.
Colour Reproduction by Scantrans Pte Ltd, Singapore.
Produced by Mandarin Offset
Printed and bound in Hong Kong.

CONTENTS

Introduction

There are few occupations more rewarding than making things for small children. Whether you sew, embroider, do woodwork or paint, there is something in this book for you.

Sooner or later, most parents realise that children need surroundings, toys and equipment all of their own. If you can provide some of these by making them yourself, you will save a great deal of money, as well as having the satisfaction of having created something different for your child.

Many parents today feel that they have no time for crafts. The problems of establishing a secure home and providing one's children with the upbringing that will equip them for life in the 21st century, take priority. This is understandable. It is quicker to dash into the local shop and buy coverlets, wall hangings, counting panels, pictures and other accessories. The things you can buy are good quality and well-made and we

should not deprecate them. But, until you have made something yourself, you are missing one of the most satisfying feelings in the world.

Children react in a most reassuring way to something you have made for them. If your expertise is not all you might want it to be, children are far from critical. You made it especially for them. That is what matters most. Fathers come into their own with hand-made toys. Even if a man feels that he is the most thumb-fingered of individuals when it comes to handling wood, the pleasure of seeing the wide-eyed wonder of a child given something that Daddy made himself, is not to be missed.

The arrival of a new baby is a good opportunity for giving presents and hand-

made gifts are always greatly appreciated on these occasions. Mothers rarely have enough time, before or after the birth, to make quilts and other nursery furnishings, so this is where relatives – and friends – come in. If you are a grandmother, mother, aunt, sister, cousin or an affectionate friend, you will find lots of things in this book that make marvellous gifts. Whatever your interest, decorative sewing, embroidery, painting, stencilling or toymaking, there is something here for you.

Toys – and things

The first chapter, Playtime, has some exciting ideas for toys. Some are quick to do and can be completed in a few hours. Others take more time. But they are all very simple to make, using only basic techniques – and I have made them at least twice myself, to ensure that there are no hidden pitfalls. The rag book is really fun to do and you will have a lot of pleasure in making this. Bright and colourful, with some amusing ideas in it, the rag book provides practice for small hands in tying bows, fastening zippers and press fasteners and coping with buttons and buttonholes – important skills when a child begins to dress himself. There is a play mat in the chapter also, very fishy with a sea, seashore, sunfish rattles and a starfish hand puppet.

For older children, a farmyard scene, complete with animals, birds and farm folk, will provide hours of amusement – and they will learn to count at the same time.

For woodwork enthusiasts, the rocking hen toy will make a very special gift and provides a lasting source of fun for children as they grow. The push-along pigeon will entertain babies when they are learning to walk, as well as toddlers.

Perfect gifts

The chapter Gifts and mementoes has some delightful things to make and in a variety of crafts. The pretty baby slippers are easy enough for beginners to make and the cross stitch picture of ducks is something even older children could attempt.

Nurseries are ideal locations for stencilling – beds, chairs, tables and doors – as well as walls – lend themselves very well to this easy and impressive technique. The pattern of shepherd and sheep is suitable for both boys and girls' rooms. All the knowhow for this fascinating craft is in the last chapter Better techniques.

I had so much fun in writing this book because I enjoy making things for babies (especially as I am a new grandmother myself). I hope that you will get as much pleasure out of Nursery Crafts as I have done in creating the projects.

ONE

Playtime

Patchwork ball

This fascinating play ball is made from fabric segments stuffed and sewn together. Babies love these balls because they are so easy for little hands to hold.

Materials
Tracing paper
8 × 45in (20 × 115cm) piece of plain fabric
  (inner sections)
6 × 45in (15 × 115cm) piece of patterned
  fabric (outer sections)
Washable polyester toy filling
Strong buttonhole thread

Preparation
1 Trace the pattern for the outer section.
Draw and cut out a paper circle 7¼in
(18.5cm) diameter. Cut the circle in half
for the inner section pattern. (A ¼in
(6mm) seam allowance is included on the
patterns.) Cut 12 inner sections from
plain fabric and 12 outer sections from
patterned fabric.

Working the design
2 With right sides facing, fold an inner
section in half. Stitch along the straight
edges about half way.

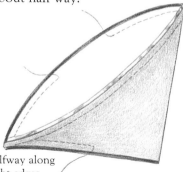

Stitch halfway along
the straight edges.

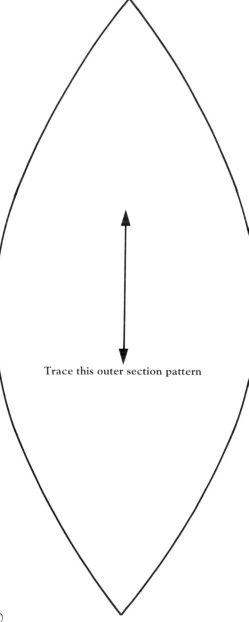

Trace this outer section pattern

3 Pin and baste the edges of the outer
section to the inner section. Starting in
the middle of a side, machine-stitch all
round. Turn to the right side and stuff
the segment firmly. Oversew to close the
opening. Repeat with all the segments.

Finishing

4 Take 2 segments and, using buttonhole thread, join them with a $\frac{3}{8}$in (9mm) buttonhole bar (A-B). Join 2 more (C-D) in the same way, between A and B, but this time interweave the two buttonhole bars at the centre.

5 Join the outer points of the segments in the same way with buttonhole bars. Join four more segments to the first four, placing them at right angles. Interweave the buttonhole bars at the centre and outer points. Join in the four remaining segments.

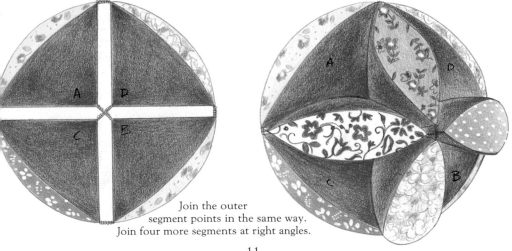

Join the outer
segment points in the same way.
Join four more segments at right angles.

Rag book

Small children are fascinated by colourful rag books which help them to learn about buttons and button holes, press fasteners, zip fasteners and simple ties.

Materials

Squared pattern paper
Light-weight iron-on interfacing
Pieces of plain fabric in jade, green, yellow and blue, each 11 × 18in (28 × 45cm)
Scraps of brightly coloured, plain and patterned fabrics
Pieces of coloured felt
Trimmings: ricrac braid, ribbons, lace etc
Stranded embroidery cottons
Washable polyester toy filling
12in (30cm) strip of touch-and-hold fastening

Fabric writing pens
Narrow green satin ribbon
Red ribbon
3 large buttons
12 large press fasteners
Small strip of thin cardboard
Light-weight green zip fastener, 7in (18cm) long
Sew-in, medium weight interfacing, 33 × 36in (88 × 90cm)
Sew-in, heavyweight interfacing, $8\frac{1}{2}$ × 18in (21 × 45cm)
Large button (for cover tab)

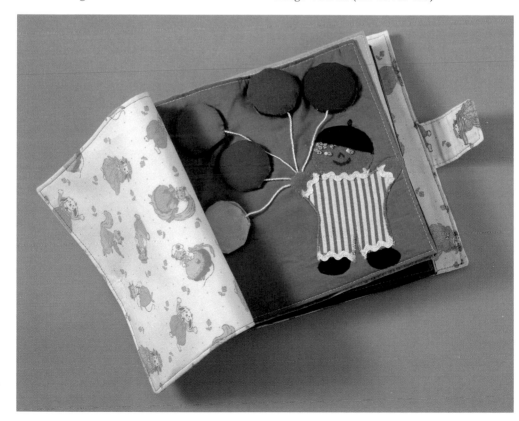

Preparation

1 Draw the pattern pieces on squared paper, working on the fold where indicated on the pattern piece. Identify the various segments as indicated on the patterns. Cut out.

2 Iron light-weight interfacing onto the wrong side of any fabrics which might fray. Spread the fabric pieces for pairs of pages 1 and 8 (jade), 2 and 7 (green), 3 and 6 (yellow) and 4 and 5 (blue). Measure and mark the page area on each piece, 9in (23cm) deep by 16½in (43cm) wide, using chalk. This includes a ¼in (6mm) turning all round.

Working the design

3 PAGE 1 BALLOON SELLER: Spread the jade fabric for pages 1 and 8. Page 1 is on the right-hand side. Using the balloon seller pattern, cut the entire shape in striped fabric then the head and hands from pink felt, and the boots and beret from blue felt.

4 Machine-appliqué the balloon seller to the right-hand corner, about ½in (1cm) inside the chalked outline. Sew on the felt face, hands and boots and beret. Embroider the features, trim with ricrac braid.

5 Cut five 1½in (4cm)-diameter circles

from different coloured fabrics for balloon bases. Machine-appliqué the circles to the background fabric (refer to the picture for positions).

6 Cut 2 circles, each 2⅜in (6cm) diameter, from the same colour fabrics, for the balloons. Make up the balloons, using the detached appliqué technique. Sew the ball part of the press fasteners to the balloon bases and the other part to the backs of the balloons. Fix the balloons in place then attach a length of coloured thread to each balloon with the other end fixed to the hand. Write 'Match my colours' on the background, using a fabric pen.

7 OPPOSITE PAGE (8) Cut 2 flower shapes from each of three fabrics, yellow, red and orange. Cut 4 green leaves. From flowered fabric, cut a window box 1¼ × 6¼in (3 × 16cm).

8 Machine-appliqué the window box near to the bottom edge of the page. Appliqué a 3½in (9cm) piece of narrow green ribbon up from the middle for the flower stem and attach a leaf on each side, at an angle (refer to the picture). Appliqué the remaining two leaves across the corners of the window box.

9 Place pairs of flowers together, wrong

Scale: 1 sq = 1in (2.5cm)

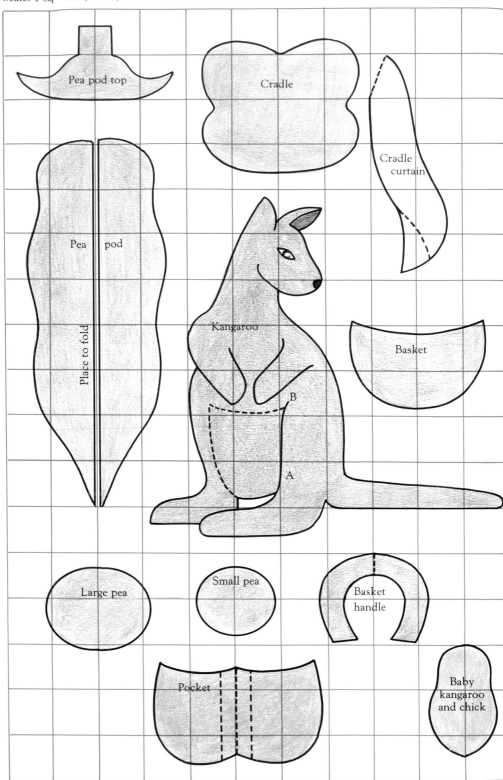

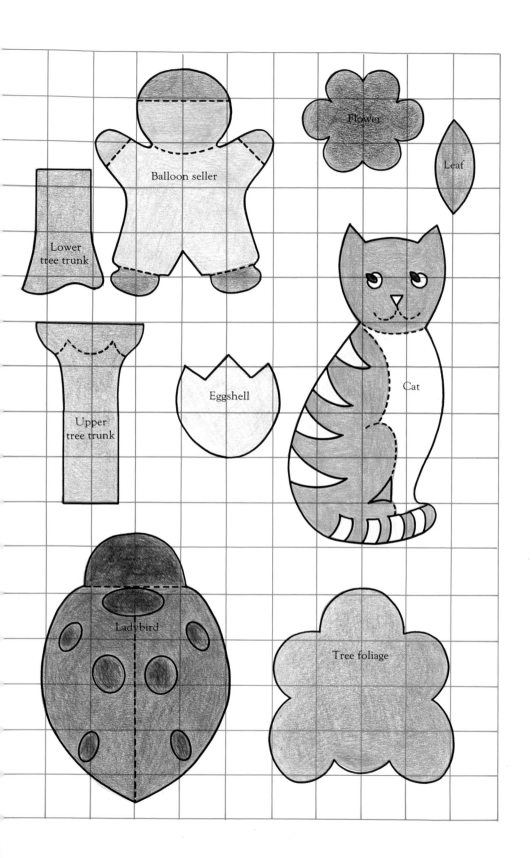

sides facing, and work machine satin stitch round the edges. Work a buttonhole in each flower. Sew buttons onto the page. Button on the flowers. Write 'Button the flowers' in fabric pen.

10 PAGES 2 AND 7 (GREEN): The cat design is on the left-hand side. Using the pattern, cut the cat body from orange fabric, then the stripes, stomach and features from cream fabric. Baste the middle of a 20in (50cm) length of red ribbon under the cat's neck. Appliqué the details to the cat and the cat to the background. Embroider the eyes in detached chain stitch, the mouth in running stitch and the whiskers in straight stitch. Write 'Tie the bow'.

11 PAGE 7: (Right-hand page.) Cut the ladybird body in red fabric and the head in black fabric. Cut the spots from black felt. Appliqué the ladybird to the background fabric, then add the head and spots. Embroider the legs in chain stitch and running stitch and the feelers in straight stitch. Work the eyes and wing line in running stitch. Write 'Count the spots' in fabric pen.

12 PAGES 3 AND 6: Work page 3 (apple tree) on the right-hand side of the fabric piece. Cut 2 upper tree trunks and 1

lower trunk. Cut 1 basket handle. Cut 12 red felt apples each ¾in (2cm) in diameter. Cut 2 baskets and 2 tree tops. Cut 1 yellow fabric pocket (to hold the lower tree trunk) 2½ × 7in (6 × 18cm).

13 BASKET: Machine-appliqué the basket handle to the lower right hand corner of the page. Stitch 2 basket pieces together, right sides facing, leaving a gap for turning. Turn to the right side. Oversew to close the seam. Machine-stitch the basket to the background, below the basket handle, so that the basket forms a pouch.

14 TREE: The upper trunk pulls up out of the pocket. Stitch the upper tree trunks to the foliage, underlapping the trunks. With wrong sides facing, place the foliage pieces together and work narrow machine satin stitch round the edges, leaving a gap. Stuff the foliage lightly and continue stitching to close the gap. Cut a piece of cardboard ¾ × 6in (2 × 15cm) and slide it up into the tree trunk to stiffen it. Stitch the bottom edge of the tree trunk.

15 POCKET: Appliqué the lower tree trunk centrally to one end of the pocket piece (about ¼in (6mm) from the short end). Right sides facing, fold the pocket

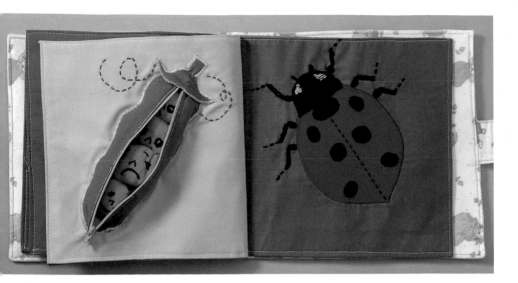

n half widthways and stitch to within ¼in (6mm) of the edges, leaving a gap for turning. Turn to the right side. Top-stitch the pocket to the page beside the basket, leaving the upper edge open. Slip the stiffened tree trunk inside the pocket. Catch the bottom corners of the trunk inside the pocket with sufficient length of thread to enable it to be pulled up.

16 APPLES: Oversew the felt apples together in pairs. Sew the ball part of the press fasteners to the foliage and the other half to the apples. Sew narrow ribbons to the apples and fasten the ribbon ends inside the basket. Embroider flowers and leaves under the tree and basket. Write 'Pick the apples' on the page using fabric pen.

17 PAGE 6: This is on the left-hand side of the yellow pages 3 and 6. Cut 1 pea pod top. Cut 4 small peas and 4 larger ones, adding ¼in (6mm) all round. Cut 2 pea pod halves from folded fabric, placing the straight edge of the pattern on the fold.

18 Stitch the zip fastener between the folded edges of the pea pod halves, placing the top of the zipper at the rounded end. Stitch the edges together below the point.

19 Place two matching pea pieces together, right sides facing and stitch round, leaving a gap. Stuff and close the gap. Embroider faces on the peas.

20 Pin the peas inside the pod, place the pod on the page and mark round the edges with chalk. Remove the pod and stitch one side of a 6in (15cm) strip of touch-and-hold fastening down the middle of the pod outline. Cut the other side into 4 pieces and sew to the backs of the peas. Work narrow machine satin stitch round the edges of the pea pod to appliqué it to the page. Work satin stitch round the pod top. Pin it in place, appliqué the top to the page. Put the peas in the pod and zip up. Write 'Put the peas in the pod' using fabric pen.

21 PAGES 4 AND 5 (BLUE): The kangaroo design is on the left and the cradle is on the right. Cut out the entire kangaroo. Adding seam allowance, cut 2 kangaroo pockets and 2 kangaroo babies. Appliqué the kangaroo to the page. Sew a small piece of touch-and-hold fastening to the kangaroo in the pocket position. Embroider the details on the kangaroo chest with straight stitches. Make up the pocket. Machine-appliqué to the kangaroo along A-B. Slipstitch round the curved edge.

22 Make up two kangaroo baby pieces, stuff and embroider the features. Sew on felt ears. Sew the other side of the touch-and-hold strip to the back of the baby. Pop into the pocket.

23 PAGE 5: Cut 2 cradle curtains, reversing the pattern for one. Adding ⅛in (6mm) seam allowance, cut 2 chicks, 2 eggshells and 2 cradles. Appliqué the cradle curtains to the right-hand side of the page and add a lace motif to top centre (refer to the picture). Sew one side of a small piece of touch-and-hold fastening to the page for the cradle and eggshell positions (refer to the picture). Stitch 2 pieces of cradle together, right sides facing, leaving a gap. Do the same with the eggshell pieces. Work a stem stitch edge to the cradle. Slipstitch the cradle to the page, overlapping the curtain edges. Slipstitch the eggshell to the left of the cradle.

24 PAGE 5: Make up the chick and stuff it. Embroider the eyes and sew on a felt beak. Sew one side of a piece of touch-and-hold fastening to the back of the chick. Write 'Put the baby to bed' across pages 4 and 5, using a fabric pen.

Finishing
25 Press the work on the wrong side, trim the pages back to the chalked outlines. Cut medium weight interfacing ⅛in (6mm) smaller all round and baste to the wrong side of the pages. Turn and press the page edges to the wrong side. Pin and baste page 2 and 7 to the back of pages 1 and 8 and top-stitch all round. Top-stitch pages 3 and 6 to pages 4 and 5.

26 FASTENING TAB: Cut a piece of heavyweight non-woven interfacing 1½ × 2½in (4 × 6cm) and a piece of the cover fabric 1½ × 6in (4 × 15cm). Fold the fabric in half widthways with right sides facing and join the two long edges, taking a ⅛in (6mm) seam. Turn to the right side and insert the interfacing. Work a buttonhole on the folded end of the tab and top-stitch all round the edges, except the open end.

27 COVER: Cut 2 pieces of fabric each 9¼ × 19in (23.5 × 48cm), and a piece of heavyweight interfacing to the same size. Place the fabric pieces together with right sides facing and pin the interfacing on top. Stitch round through all thicknesses leaving one short side open for turning. Turn to the right side and press in the opening edges ⅛in (6mm). Tuck the raw end of the tab underneath the middle of the edge and baste, then top-stitch. Arrange the pages in order and stitch down the spine. Sew a button on the cover. Finish with a ribbon bow.

Farmyard counting panel

This cheerful wall hanging for the nursery is not only decorative and amusing but will help a small child to learn to count. Hang it where it can be reached easily.

Materials

Squared pattern paper

24 × 33in (60 × 84cm) piece of pelmet-weight non-woven interfacing

12 × 33in (30 × 84cm) piece of blue fabric (sky, section 9)

Pieces of plain and patterned fabric for the fields, garden, house etc (refer to the picture)

½yd (45cm) each of white and green ricrac braid

Pieces of coloured felt (including beige, white and black)

Stranded embroidery cottons

39in (1m) of ⅞in (2cm)-wide touch-and-hold fastening

Washable polyester toy filling

24 × 33in (60 × 84cm) piece of fabric for backing

39in (1m) of ½in (1cm)-diameter wooden dowelling

45in (115cm) of·1in (2.5cm)-wide ribbon

Preparation

1 Draw the pattern of the farmyard layout on squared paper. Number the sections and cut them apart. Pin each section to its relevant fabric and cut out with ¼in (6mm) seam allowance all round.

2 Draw the figures, animals and bird patterns on squared paper. Cut out the patterns. Using them, cut the basic shape twice, once from coloured felt (see the patterns for a guide) and once from beige felt. Some of the figures are reversed left to right for variety.

3 Still using the patterns, cut the appliqué pieces from felt (the children's clothes, the cows' spots, noses and hooves, tree foliage, apples and leaves etc). Baste, then sew in place.

Make a farmyard game

First, prepare the farmyard layout on a piece of stiff board, using coloured papers instead of fabric. Make the animals and figures in card and paper also. Make a set for each player. On the farmyard layout, stick numbers from **1** to **12**, with the farmhouse position as **12**. Stick numbers on the figures and animals.

To play, two dice are thrown and the player decides which of the figures or animals he will position on the farmyard. He can add the two dice together to make a single number (ie two sixes to make the twelve for the farmhouse) or he can use the individual dice numbers to place two pieces. The winner is the first player to have placed all his pieces, the others counting the pieces left over against their score.

The skill lies in deciding how to use the dice numbers. For instance, a player may have positioned the farmhouse with 12, and then is unable to throw sixes, which is the number for the sheep. He could be left with 3 pieces, instead of just one.

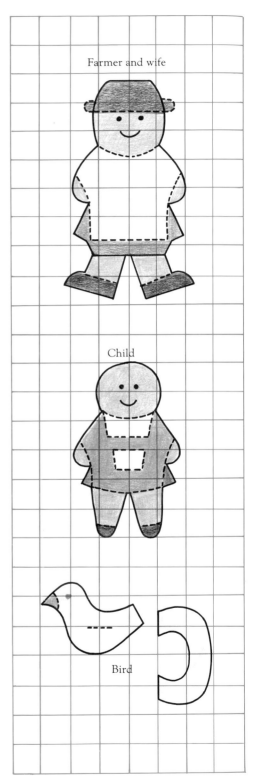

Farmer and wife

Child

Bird

Scale: 1 sq = ½in (1cm)

Farmhouse

Hen

Cow

Flower

Pig

Apple tree

Sheep

Working the design

4 Press under the edges of the sections. Baste them to the interfacing background, edges touching. Set the sewing machine to a zigzag and work round the pieces, except the outside edges. Straight-stitch round the outside edges.

5 Stitch white ricrac braid around section 2. Stitch pieces of green ricrac braid to section 6. Embroider grass in straight and fly stitches.

6 Work cream detached chain and fly stitches over section 8. Work white straight stitch clouds on section 9 and white French knot flowers with green fly stitch leaves on section 4.

7 Draw 10 circles 1¼in (3cm) diameter on white felt and embroider the numerals 1–10 in black chain stitches. Cut out and slipstitch each numbered circle to its section.

Scale. 1 sq – 1in (2.5cm)

8 FIGURES AND ANIMALS: Place felt pieces together with the beige shape at the back and oversew together, leaving a gap. Stuff, close the gap. Embroider the details (features etc) and then sew on the animal's heads. Cut small pieces of touch-and-hold fastening and sew one side to the backs of the figures, animals and birds. Sew the other side to the farmyard sections (refer to the picture).

Finishing

9 Fold the edges of the backing fabric to the wrong side. Slipstitch to the back along the top edge. Machine-stitch 1½in (4cm) below to make a casing for the rod. Slipstitch the backing to the panel all round. Insert the dowelling. Tie the ribbon ends to the dowelling.

Sewing on trimmings
Ricrac braid Machine-stitch to the fabric working down the middle of the braid.
Ribbon Machine-stitch down both edges, working in the same direction.

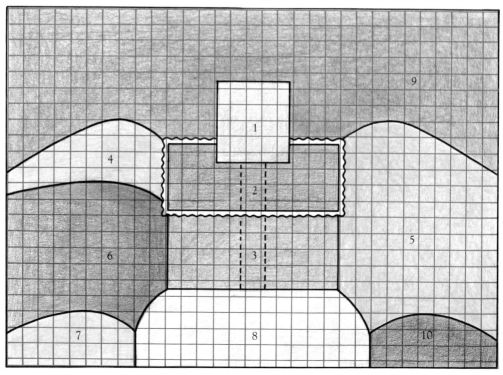

Rocking hen toy

Simple woodworking skills are all that this cheerful toy requires. The decoration provides scope for using bright colours which all small children love.

Materials

Squared pattern paper
7ft (2.15m) of ¾in (2cm)-thick pine wood
6in (15cm) of ½in (1cm) ramin dowelling
Sandpaper in coarse, medium and fine
  grades
Wood glue
8 countersunk wood screws, 1¼in (3.5cm)
2in (5cm) countersunk wood screw
Wood filler
Craft paints, yellow, red, white, blue and
  black
Satin finish polyurethane varnish

Preparation

1 Draw the patterns on squared paper.
Mark the arrows to indicate the grain of
wood. Using the patterns, mark on the
wood 2 rockers, 2 side heads, 1 centre
head and 1 tail. Mark 1 seat piece with
the back end of the seat (A-B) cut at a 45°
angle (see pattern). Cut 1 front section.

Working the design

2 Cut the various pieces.

3 HEAD: Smooth the edges of the head
with sandpaper. Glue together the three
sections and, when the glue is dry, level
up the back and front edge, sandpapering
as necessary. Square up the lower end of
the neck and make any adjustments by
planing or sawing to ensure that the head
stands upright. Sandpaper the head
thoroughly and make a chamfer on all
edges except at the bottom where the
head fits the body.

4 HANDLES: Using a ½in (1cm) bit, drill a
¾in (18mm) hole on each side of the head
(at x on the pattern). Cut 2 pieces of
ramin dowelling each 2¾in (7cm) long and
stick a piece into each hole for handles.

5 BODY: Glue together the seat, rockers
and front section, making sure that the
angled edge of the seat is at the back,
where the tail will fit later. The front end
of the seat fits flush to the front of the
rockers and the front section. Square up
the fit of the various sections and leave
the glue to dry, under clamps if possible.

6 At the top of each rocker, drill 4 pilot
holes to take the 1¼in (3.5cm) screws.
They should be at a depth of ⅜in (9mm)
from the straight edge and evenly spaced.
The screws are countersunk so that the
heads are below the wood surface.

7 The last screw at either end will hold
the tail. Apply glue to the end of the seat
and stick the tail in place, then insert the
screws. Fill the countersunk holes with
wood filler.

Finishing

8 Sandpaper the toy thoroughly and
chamfer the edges. Stick the head to the
centre front of the body. When the glue
is dry drill a pilot hole and screw the
head to the body from the inside of the
work, using the remaining screw.

9 Dilute the craft paints with water,
paint the toy, following the picture.
Finish with a coat of polyurethane
varnish.

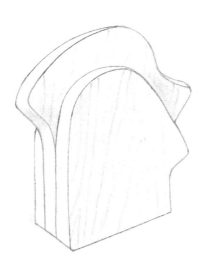

Glue the three head sections together.

Scale: 1 sq = 2in (5cm)

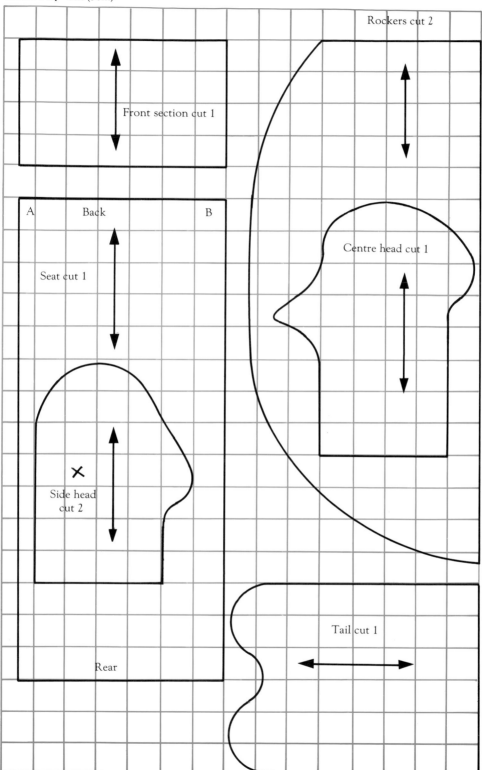

Rockers cut 2

Front section cut 1

A   Back   B

Seat cut 1

Centre head cut 1

Side head
cut 2

Rear

Tail cut 1

25

Fishy play mat

Baby will enjoy taking his exercise among the fishes on this colourful mat. It provides both interest and play. There is a starfish puppet also so that you can join in the fun.

Materials
Squared pattern paper, thin cardboard
45 × 45in (115 × 115cm) piece of dark cotton fabric (background)
Scraps of brightly coloured cotton fabrics
11 × 40in (28 × 102cm) piece of towelling (for puppet)
$19\frac{1}{2}$ × 39in (50 × 100cm) patterned or plain fabric (sea)
Scraps of felt
2 toy squeakers
Small, round mirror
4in (10cm) piece of touch-and-hold fastening
Washable polyester toy filling
5 small bells
Narrow ribbon
3 round, plastic boxes with lids
Pebbles or beads
Self-adhesive fabric tape
Stranded embroidery cottons
8 × 16in (20 × 40cm) piece of heavyweight non-woven interfacing
$19\frac{1}{2}$ × 39in (50 × 100cm) piece of fabric (shore)
5 buttons
10 × 15in (25 × 38cm) piece of felt
$3\frac{1}{4}$in (3m) of wide, white ricrac braid
39in (100cm) square of backing fabric

Preparation
1 Draw the patterns on squared paper. Transfer (or stick) the patterns to cardboard and cut out for templates.

2 Cut the background fabric to 39in (100cm) square.

3 Place the fish templates on the wrong side of the coloured fabrics and draw round 5 fish bodies and 7 tails. Cut out, allowing an extra $\frac{1}{4}$in (6mm) seam allowance all round. For 2 squeaky fish, cut 2 pairs of bodies in each of two colours, again adding seam allowance.

4 For the starfish puppet, use the templates to cut 2 starfish bodies from towelling, adding seam allowance all round. Cut 2 glove shapes also.

Working the design
5 THE SEA: Place the cardboard templates on the wrong side of the fish shapes and press the seam allowance to the wrong side. Remove the templates.

6 Lightly chalk an area of 15 × 24in (38 × 60cm) in the centre of the sea fabric, then arrange the fish in the area. Baste the 7 fish tails down first, then the 5 fish bodies, overlapping the tails. (Two tails are for the squeaker fish later.) Zigzag stitch all round the fish then work 2 vertical stripes along each. (Use a decorative stitch if your machine has one. Otherwise, work the stripes by hand.) Sew felt circles to the fish for eyes.

7 SQUEAKER FISH: On the remaining fish pieces, work 2 stripes along one body piece of each. Stitch a 2in (5cm) strip of touch-and-hold fastening down the middle of the corresponding shape. With right sides facing, join the shapes, leaving a gap. Turn to the right side, stuff lightly, inserting a squeaker, and close the gap. Stitch the corresponding lengths of touch-and-hold fastening next to the tails where the squeaky fish are to be positioned.

8 STARFISH PUPPET: Stitch the glove pieces together, leaving the wrist edge

open. Neaten all raw edges. Stitch the pieces of starfish together, leaving a gap. Turn to the right side, stuff lightly and close the gap. Sew felt eyes to the face and embroider a mouth.

9 Pin the starfish to the glove, matching fingers and starfish arms, then sew in place. Sew a bell to each starfish arm. Sew a ribbon loop to the top arm.

10 PEBBLE RATTLES: Put pebbles (or beads) into the flat, round boxes and tape

the lids on securely. Cut 2 felt circles (use pinking shears if you have them) 4½in (11cm) diameter, for each box. Sew felt eyes and embroider a mouth to the centre of one circle. Top-stitch the circles together, close to the edges.

11 To stuff the rattles, cut a slit down the centre of the back, insert the plastic container and stuff round the edges to pad. Close the slit with oversewing. Sew a ribbon loop at top centre to fit a button later.

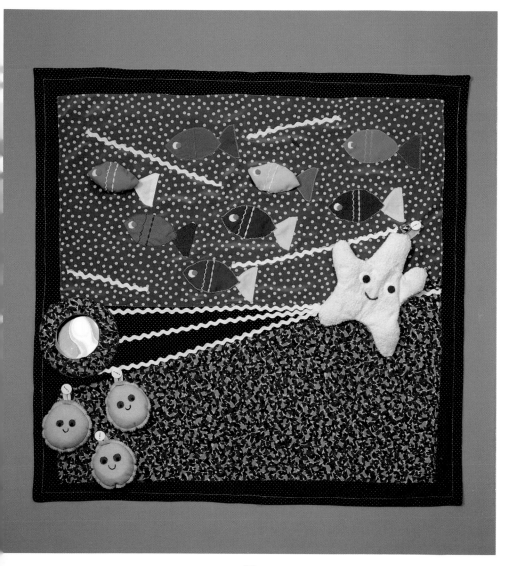

Scale: 1 sq = 1in (2.5cm)

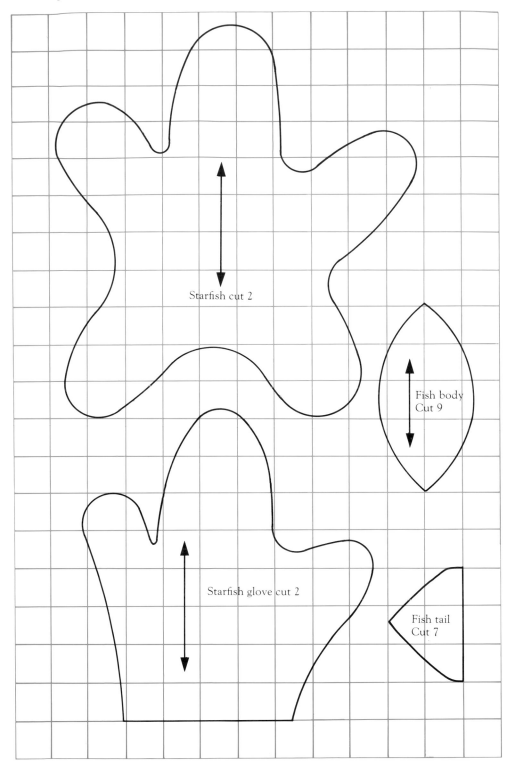

Starfish cut 2

Fish body
Cut 9

Starfish glove cut 2

Fish tail
Cut 7

12 ROCK POOL: For the upper covering of the pool, cut an 8in (20cm) circle of heavy-weight non-woven interfacing. Mark and then cut a circle from the centre 4½in (11cm) diameter.

13 Next, from the shore fabric, cut 2 circles 8¾in (22cm) diameter. Right sides facing, stitch them together, leaving a gap for turning. Turn right side out. Insert the prepared interfacing and oversew the gap. Pin the inner edges of the fabric to the edges of the hole in the interfacing. Snip a 3½in (9cm) diameter circle through both thicknesses of fabric. Snip into the edges, fold to the wrong side and oversew to neaten.

14 Gather the outer and inner edges. Draw up the outer gathering so that the diameter is contracted to 7in (18cm). Draw up the inner gathering a little.

15 ROCK POOL BACKING: Cut a 7in (18cm) circle of interfacing and cover with fabric in the same way as stages 12 and 13. Oversew the upper covering edges to the backing, leaving a gap for inserting the mirror. Make a thread loop for a button to close the gap.

16 Pin and baste the sea and shore to the background fabric, allowing a margin all round. Leave a horizontal, v-shaped space (refer to picture) so that the background fabric shows between the sea and the shore (about 7in (18cm) at the left-hand end). Cut the shore at an angle, turn a

narrow hem, top-stitch the shore to the background.

17 Cut and stitch 3 pieces of white ricrac braid to the fabric between sea and shore. Cut the remaining braid into short pieces and stitch between the fish. Sew the rock pool to the shore.

18 Sew on the buttons to hold the pebble rattles and the starfish puppet. Wrong sides facing, baste the background edges and backing fabric together. From the remaining background fabric, cut 4 facing strips each 3 × 39in (7.5 × 100cm) and face the edges of the play mat.

19 On the front, fold and stitch the facing edges in place.

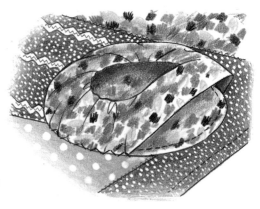

Oversew the upper covering to the backing, leaving a gap for the mirror.

29

Tiny toys

*These pretty little toys, a bunny, a pussy and a teddy,
are just the right size for a baby's hand and use only small pieces
of washable fabric.*

Materials
For each toy
Tracing pattern paper
8 × 12in (20 × 30cm) piece of soft fabric
5 × 9in (13 × 23cm) piece of patterned
    cotton fabric
Small pieces of washable fun felt
Stranded embroidery cottons
Washable polyester toy filling
In addition for the bunny
4 × 5in (10 × 13cm) piece of contrasting
    cotton fabric
1 small button
In addition for the teddy
2 small buttons

Preparation
1 Trace the pattern pieces for the toy.
Cut out and put in all the markings.
Seam allowances of ¼in (6mm) are
included.

2 Fold the soft fabric in half widthways,
right sides facing. Pin the body pattern to
the doubled fabric and cut out. Mark the
position 'X' on one body (see pattern).
Pin the ear pattern (teddy, pussy or
bunny) to doubled soft fabric and cut
out. Pin the ear pattern to doubled
patterned fabric and cut 2 ear linings. Cut
eyes and noses from felt.

Bunny
3 From patterned fabric, cut 1 waistcoat
back and 2 waistcoat fronts. Cut the
same pieces from contrasting cotton. Cut
a 1½in (37mm)-diameter circle of soft
fabric for the tail.

Pussy
4 From the patterned fabric, cut a skirt
piece 2 × 9in (5 × 23cm) and a bias-cut
strip 1½ × 6in (3 × 15cm) for a bow.

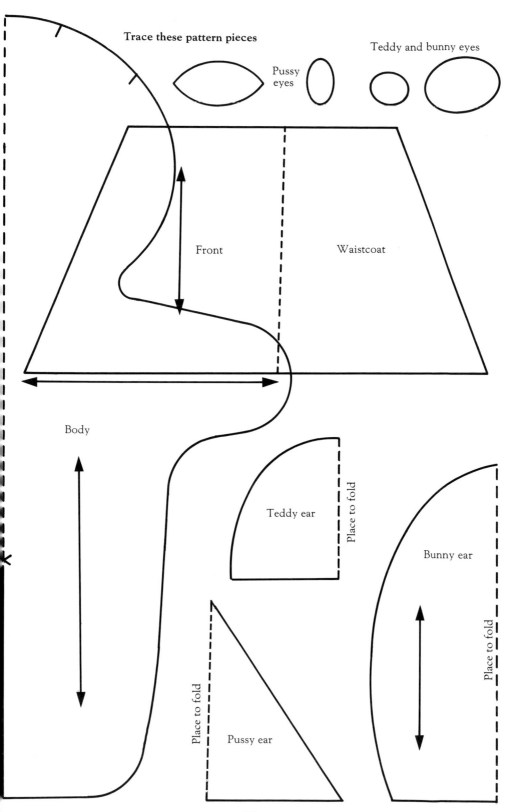

Trace these pattern pieces

Pussy eyes

Teddy and bunny eyes

Front

Waistcoat

Body

Teddy ear

Place to fold

Bunny ear

Place to fold

Place to fold

Pussy ear

Place to fold

Teddy

5 From patterned fabric, cut a piece for the trousers, 2 × 6½in (5 × 16cm). Cut a bib front 1½ × 3in (3 × 7.5cm) and 2 straps each 1 × 4in (2.5 × 10cm).

Working the design

6 EARS: For the bunny and teddy, baste a soft fabric ear to a patterned ear, right sides facing. Stitch round the curved edge, clip into the seam allowance and turn right side out. For the pussy, stitch along 2 straight sides.

7 With the patterned side of the ear facing you, fold the outer corners to the centre and baste to the right side of one body piece (see pattern).

8 Right sides facing, baste the body pieces together from A to D. Machine-stitch but do not turn yet.

9 LEGS: Mark a line on the toy body from the mark 'X' to the bottom edge. Machine-stitch on either side ⅛in (3mm) from the line. Cut along the line. Turn the toy right side out and stuff lightly. Close the gap in the seam.

Finishing

10 Sew the eyes and nose to the face. Embroider the mouth, using all 6 strands of embroidery cotton together. Add whiskers to the bunny and pussy using 2 strands of embroidery cotton.

11 BUNNY: Gather the edges of the tail circle and draw up tightly. Stuff lightly and sew to the back of the toy. With right sides facing, stitch the patterned fabric waistcoat to the contrasting fabric pieces, leaving a gap to turn. Turn to the right side and press. Pin the back and front to the toy and catch the shoulders and lower, outside corners together. Overlap the fronts at the inner corners. Sew a button in place.

12 TEDDY: On the trousers strip, press ¼in (6mm) to the wrong side on the long edges. Stitch. Join the short ends at the centre back and work a ⅜in (1cm)-wide slit for the legs (refer back to stage 9). Turn to the right side.

13 With right sides facing, fold the bib front in half, stitch round, leaving a gap and turn to the right side. Catch the unstitched edge to underlap the centre front edge of the trousers.

14 STRAPS: Press ¼in (6mm) to the wrong side on the long edges then fold the strips in half lengthways. Stitch along the edges. Catch the straps under the top of the bib front. Sew on the buttons. Slip the trousers on the teddy, cross the straps at the back and catch the ends to the back of the trousers.

15 PUSSY: Turn a narrow hem on the long edges of the skirt and join the short ends. Gather one long edge, draw up to fit the toy and catch in place. Make a bow from the bias strip (refer to stage 14 for the teddy straps). Sew the bow to the front.

Enlarging patterns

Trace-off patterns can be made larger (or smaller) simply by turning them into graph patterns. First, trace the pattern from the page. Rule lines round the shapes so that they are in a square or rectangular box. Measure and mark the box outline into 1in (2.5cm) squares.

Next, decide the size you want to enlarge the pattern to. Draw a box outline to the dimensions. Measure and mark the outline into the same number of squares as your original pattern. Then, all you have to do is copy the pattern outlines into each of the squares.

You can reduce a pattern in the same way. Simply draw a boxed area to the smaller dimensions, mark the box into the same number of squares as your original pattern, and then copy the pattern into the squares.

Push-along pigeon

This unusual toy was inspired by the way real pigeons move their heads as they walk. You could try the pattern first in strong cardboard before making the toy in wood.

Scale: 1 sq = ½in (1cm)

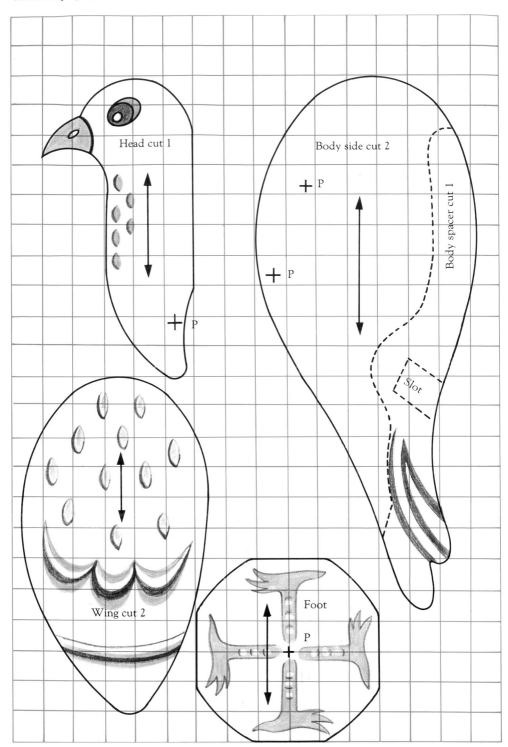

Head cut 1

Body side cut 2

P

P

P

Body spacer cut 1

Slot

Wing cut 2

Foot

P

34

Materials

Squared pattern paper
6 × 7in (15 × 18cm) piece of ⅛in (3mm)
   birch ply-wood for wings
8¾ × 13in (22 × 33cm) piece of ¼in (6mm)
   birch plywood for other parts
39in (1m) of ⅝in (15mm) diameter
   dowelling for a handle
4in (10cm) thin, stiff wire
Empty plastic food pot
Fine sandpaper; wood glue
Modeller's enamel paint

Preparation

1 Draw the pattern pieces on squared
paper. Mark the pivot points (P)
accurately.

2 Trace 2 wings onto the ⅛in (3mm) ply-
wood. Trace 2 bodies and one each of the
other shapes on ¼in (6mm) ply-wood.
Mark 2 pivot points on the outer
surfaces of the bodies (reversing one
body so that you have a pair). Mark
spacer positions on the inner surfaces of
the feet wheel and the head.

Working the design

3 Cut out all the shapes and lightly
sandpaper the edges. Sandpaper the outer
surfaces only of the 2 bodies and wings
(reversing to give a pair). Sandpaper both
surfaces of the head and feet wheel so
that they are very smooth (they must fit
loosely between the body pieces).

4 Drill the pivot holes. (Check that the
wire turns easily through the holes. If it
seems tight, use a drill bit slightly larger.)

5 Paint one surface and the edges of the
body and wing pieces, making sure that
you reverse them to make a pair. On the
body spacer, paint the edge only. Using
the wood glue, stick the inside of the
wings to the outside of the bodies.

6 Cut 4 washers from the plastic food
pot each ½in (1cm) diameter. Use these on
the pivot wires on each side of the
moving parts.

Here is how the pigeon fits together. As the
wheel rotates it makes the head move
back and forth.

7 Cut 2 pivot wires each ¾in (18mm)
long. Push the wires through the drilled
holes on one body side so that they
project on the inside. Place the head and
feet wheel over the pivots. Hold the body
side vertically and check that rotating the
wheel moves the head to and fro.

8 Hold the body spacer in position on
the same body piece. Check that the head
still moves freely. When you are
satisfied, the spacer may be stuck to the
inside of the body piece. Fit the other
side of the body over the pivot wires.
Hold the body firmly together and check
that the head and feet wheel move freely.
Any slight stiffness can be reduced by
sanding them down a little more.

9 Remove the head and the feet wheel
and paint them. When completely dry,
replace them in position. Stick the
second body piece in place.

Finishing

10 Shape the end of the handle and stick
the end into the slot in the body spacer.

Small wooden toys

Inexpensive kitchen items, pepper mills and egg-cups, are easily adapted to make dolls and a rattle. Here is a simple way to make wooden toys without having to do the wood work!

PEPPER MILL DOLLS
Materials
For each doll
Small, wooden pepper mill
Fine and coarse sandpaper
2¼in (5.5cm) of ¼in (6mm) dowelling
Modeller's enamel paints
Strong thread
Coloured wooden beads, different sizes and shapes
Wood glue
Clear varnish
6in (15cm) length of round elastic
In addition for the little man
Wooden cotton reel
2¼in (5.5cm) of ¼in (6mm) dowelling
Additional tool
Drill

Preparation
1 FOR BOTH DOLLS: Unscrew the knob of the pepper mill and remove the wooden head. Unscrew the grinder. Discard all the metal parts.

2 Using coarse sandpaper, smooth the finish from the wooden head until the bare wood is exposed. Smooth off with fine sandpaper.

Working the design
3 FOR BOTH DOLLS: Using a ⅜in (9mm) drill bit, bore two equally spaced holes either side of the top of the pepper mill, each about ½in (1cm) from the upper edge. With a finer drill bit bore another hole ¼in (6mm) above the holes for arms (to take the elastic later).

4 Now bore a hole at each end of the piece of dowelling to take the thread for the arms.

5 LITTLE MAN: Bore holes through the other piece of dowelling for the doll's legs. Saw one end from the cotton reel for a hat.

6 LITTLE WOMAN: Bore two more parallel holes, approximately ⅜in (1cm) apart in the centre of the dowelling for the arms. These take the thread for the legs.

7 Paint the features and hair on the head piece, the rest of the mill for the body, and the little man's cotton reel hat. Paint the dowel pieces. Leave to dry thoroughly.

Bore holes in the pepper mill. Bore 2 more holes in the dowelling for the little woman.

36

and the little man's cotton reel hat. Paint the dowel pieces. Leave to dry thoroughly.

Finishing
8 LITTLE MAN: Insert the arms dowel through the holes. Thread a needle with about 12in (30cm) of thread and double it. Tie a small bead about 2in (5cm) from the ends, then string on a square bead for the hand and then continue for the arms, varying the colours and sizes. Push the needle through the hole in the dowel and through one more small bead, then go back through the beads already strung. Tie off the threads firmly below the first bead. Dab the knot with adhesive then trim the ends. Repeat for the other arm.

9 Insert the other piece of dowel for the legs and string on beads in the same way. Varnish the head and leave to dry. Roughen the underside of the cotton reel hat and stick it to the head. Stick the head to the body. Thread elastic through the small holes at the top of the body and tie in a loop.

10 LITTLE WOMAN: Insert the dowel for the arms through the appropriate holes and string the beads for the legs. Push the needle up through one of the holes near the centre of the dowel. Insert the needle downwards through the next hole and string beads for the other leg, in the reverse order. Adjust the length of the thread, tie off, secure with adhesive and trim the ends. String the arms as for the Little man doll.

11 Varnish the head and leave to dry. Using coarse sandpaper, flatten the base of a bead for her hair bun. Thread a needle and double the thread, tying a small bead near to the end. Insert the needle through the hole on the inside of the head (which held the discarded metal rod) push the needle up through the top of the head, through the bead and back down. Before adjusting and securing the thread end, dab adhesive to the flattened part of the bead.

12 Thread an elastic loop through the holes, as for the Little man.

EGG-CUPS RATTLE
Materials
2 wooden egg-cups
6in (15cm) piece of ⅜in (9mm) dowelling
Assorted coloured wooden beads
Modeller's enamel paints
Strong thread
Coarse sandpaper
Small bell (or other rattle object)
Wood glue

Preparation
1 On one egg-cup, drill a hole to fit the dowel through the middle of the base (this will be the face).

2 Drill a smaller hole through the centre base of the other egg-cup (this will be the hat).

Working the design
3 Paint the hat and the dowel. Paint the face.

4 When the paint is dry, stick the dowel into the face egg cup. Stick a large bead on the other end of the dowel.

5 HAT TASSEL: Thread a needle with a length of strong thread. Thread on a bead with a large hole near to the thread end. Working from inside the hat egg-cup, push the needle up through the hole and thread on a 3in (7.5cm) length of beads. Re-insert the needle through the last bead but one and back through the beads. Pass the needle to the inside of the egg-cup and through the retaining bead. Tighten the thread, then string another length of beads in the same way. Repeat to make 5 tassel strands. Tie the thread ends and secure with a dab of adhesive before trimming the ends.

6 Using sandpaper, roughen the rim of both egg-cups. Put the bell or rattle inside one of them, then stick the egg-cups together.

Geese pram toy

Babies will love this little toy, fixed across the pram or crib. Use washable, colourfast felt for the beaks, feet and eyes. You could string coloured wooden beads between the geese.

Materials
Tracing pattern paper
6 × 36in (15 × 90cm) piece of white cotton towelling
Washable polyester toy filling
8in (20cm) square of orange fun felt
Scraps of blue fun felt
White stranded embroidery cotton

1yd (1m) approximately of ⅛in (3mm)-wide satin ribbon
Round elastic (optional)

Preparation
1 Trace the pattern on pattern paper. Cut out the body and wing pieces have ¼in (6mm) seam allowances included.

40

Trace these pattern pieces.

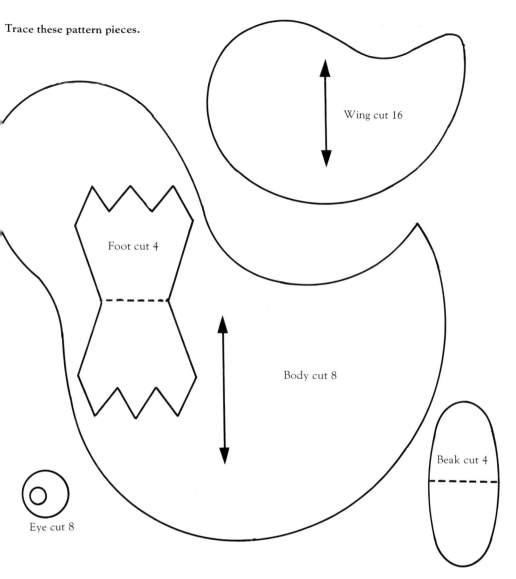

Wing cut 16

Foot cut 4

Body cut 8

Beak cut 4

Eye cut 8

2 Pin the patterns to fabric and cut out 8 bodies and 16 wings. From orange fun felt, cut 4 beaks and 4 pairs of feet. From blue fun felt, cut 8 circles for eyes.

Working the design
3 Stitch the bodies together in pairs, right sides facing, leaving a gap for turning. Turn to the right side and stuff lightly. Close the gaps.

4 Make up the wings in the same way but do not stuff. Sew the wings to the bodies.

5 Fold the beaks and feet in half and sew to the bodies so that 2 geese face to the right and 2 face to the left. Sew on the eyes and embroider a French knot on each eye.

6 Thread the ribbon on a sharp, large-eyed needle. Pass the needle through each of the geese. Attach elastic loops to the ends if desired.

Caterpillar toy

A colourful pull-along toy that will delight any toddler. You will enjoy making it because only very simple woodcraft techniques are involved.

Materials
Glass paper
11in (28cm) piece of $2\frac{1}{8} \times 1\frac{3}{4}$in ($3 \times 4.5$cm) pine (body)
$1\frac{3}{4}$in (4.5cm) square of pine wood (head)
8in (20cm) piece of pine, $\frac{5}{8} \times \frac{5}{8}$in (15mm × 15mm)
18in (45cm) length of expanding curtain wire
Wood glue
7in (18cm) piece of 1in (2.5cm) dowelling
24in (60cm) piece of $\frac{1}{4}$in (6mm) dowelling
2 smaller beads (nose and tail)
Modeller's enamel paints
Small screw eye
11 large, coloured wooden beads
Cord

Preparation
1 Smooth off all the pieces of wood.

2 Round off the edges of the body piece of wood then cut into nine $1\frac{1}{4}$in (3cm) pieces. Round off the edges of the head piece.

3 Drill a hole through the centre of one of the 9 body pieces, so that the curtain wire slips through easily. Hold the drilled piece against an undrilled piece and mark the position of the hole with the drill bit. Drill all the pieces with a hole. Number the pieces as you drill them.

4 Drill a hole about $\frac{3}{4}$in (18mm) deep in the centre of one side of the head piece. Drill 2 holes diagonally into the front top edge of the head piece for inserting the feelers later.

5 Take the third piece of wood and, starting $\frac{5}{8}$in (15mm) from one end, drill 6 holes to take the $\frac{1}{4}$in (6mm) dowelling loosely. Space each so that it is $1\frac{1}{4}$in (3cm) away from the previous hole. Saw the wood into 9 $1\frac{1}{4}$in (3cm) pieces so that a hole is in the centre of each.

6 String the body pieces on the curtain wire temporarily and decide which of the sides will be the under body. Stick one of the drilled pieces you prepared in stage 5 underneath each of five body segments. Stick one under the head segment. Remove the pieces from the wire.

7 WHEELS: Cut 12 wheels $\frac{1}{2}$in (1cm) thick from the 1in (2.5cm) dowelling. Smooth with glass paper. Drill a $\frac{1}{4}$in (6mm) hole through the centre of each. Using pencil compasses, draw a 1in (2.5cm) circle on paper. Cut out and use this as a pattern to mark the centre of the wheels. Paint the wheels.

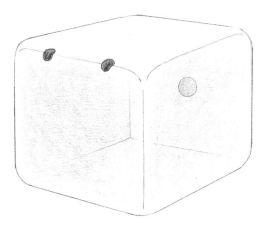

Drill a hole about $\frac{3}{4}$in (18mm) deep in one side of the head piece. Drill holes for the two feelers.

42

8 Cut 6 pieces each 2¾in (7cm) from the ¼in (6mm) dowelling. Stick a wheel on one end of each piece. Thread the dowel through the hole under the body pieces and the head piece. Stick on the other wheel.

9 HEAD: Paint the toy. Paint the face. Stick on a bead for the nose. Insert the screw eye in the lower front. Cut two 2¾in (7cm) pieces of dowelling and stick them into the holes in the head. Stick beads onto the ends for feelers.

10 Glue a small bead onto one end of the curtain wire for a tail. Thread on a wheeled body piece, a bead and then a body piece in that order to the head. Stick the wire end into the drilled head. Attach a cord to the screw eye.

Cut two wheels, drill holes in the centre. Stick a wheel on one end of the dowel.

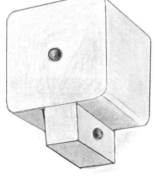

Cut six underbody pieces with a hole drilled in each.

Stick the drilled underbody pieces under the body segments

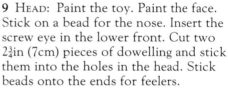
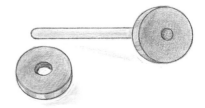

TWO
Gifts and Mementoes

Jungle quilt

Down in the jungle something stirs — is it a tiger, a crocodile or a monkey? Perhaps it is an exotic bird? Think of the fun the children are going to have with this quilt!

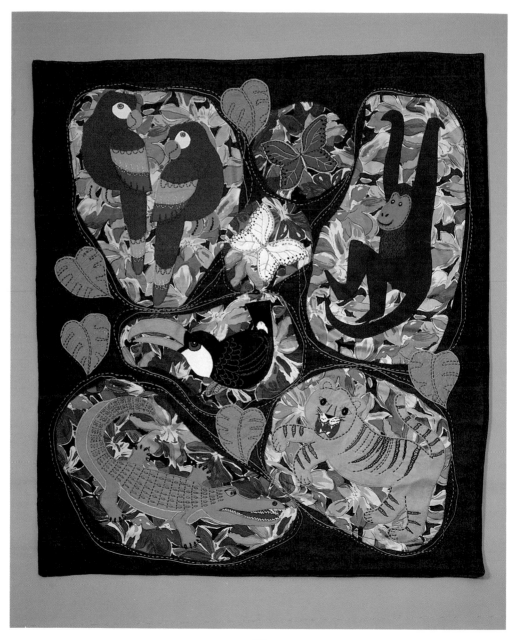

Materials

Squared pattern paper, thin cardboard
20 × 36in (50 × 90cm) piece of light weight
    fusible interfacing
24 × 36in (60 × 90cm) piece of printed
    fabric
16 × 36in (40 × 90cm) piece of printed
    fabric
24 × 20in (60 × 50cm) piece of jade fabric
    (crocodile, leaves)
14 × 20in (35 xx 50cm) piece of yellow
    fabric (tiger, details)
10 × 22in (25 × 55cm) piece of purple
    fabric (monkey)
10 × 16in (15 × 40cm) piece of white
    fabric (toucan, butterfly, details)
10in (25cm) square of black fabric
    (toucan)
16in (40cm) square of red fabric (parrots'
    details)
Small pieces of fabric, royal blue, ginger
    brown, yellow-green (details)
Stranded embroidery cottons
39 × 45in (100 × 115cm) piece of fabric
    (quilt front)
39 × 45in (100 × 115cm) piece of polyester
    wadding
39 × 45in (100 × 115cm) piece of lining
Note: It is recommended that you use
washable polyester/cotton fabrics and
all-purpose sewing threads.

Preparation

1 Draw the patterns on squared paper.
Stick to thin cardboard and cut out.

Here is a project for children. Fix a
large piece of cardboard to the wall
and sponge-paint a jungle, black near
the bottom and merging through
dark greens and mid-greens to yellow
at the top. Stick knitting wool to
paper tree trunks. Stick twisted wool
between the trees for creepers. Cut
leaf shapes and butterflies from
coloured papers. Cut the creatures
from thin card and stick coloured
paper to them to simulate fur,
feathers and scales. Stick everything
to the board.

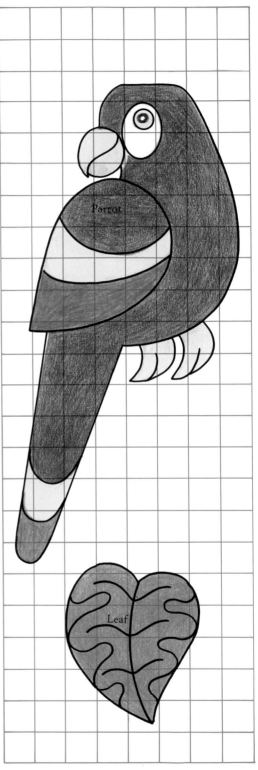

2 Place the templates on the adhesive side of the fusible interfacing and draw round each shape. Then draw a ⅛in (3mm) seam allowance on the edges of each. Mark out 2 parrots (reversing one), 5 leaves (reversing two), and 2 butterflies. Draw 1 monkey, 1 crocodile, 1 toucan and 1 tiger. Cut out roughly round each shape.

3 Place the shiny side of the interfacing shapes on the wrong side of the relevant fabrics (refer to the picture). Steam-press to fuse. Press interfacing to the wrong side of the details fabrics.

4 Baste each of the shapes to the background fabric, making sure that there is about 3in (7.5cm) surplus round each shape.

Working the design
5 Machine-appliqué round the shapes, using satin stitch.

6 Using the templates, cut the details of each figure from the relevant fabrics (refer to the picture). Baste them in position, then machine-appliqué onto the printed fabric.

7 Work the detail embroidery on the figures, following the picture and using either free-style or machine embroidery.

8 When the embroidery is complete, cut roughly round each piece of appliqué, press the edges to the wrong side and pin, then baste, to the front quilt piece. Work narrow, open machine satin stitch round the edges.

Toucan

Monkey

9 Using jade thread, work a line of narrow open satin stitch at random near the edges of the shapes. Follow with a line of running stitches, using doubled thread.

10 Appliqué the leaves directly onto the quilt, then embroider the details in running stitch.

Finishing

11 With right sides facing, place the lining fabric on top of the wadding. Wrong sides facing, pin the quilt front on the lining fabric, matching raw edges. Baste. Stitch the edges through all thicknesses, taking a $\frac{1}{4}$in (6mm) seam, and leaving a gap for turning.

12 Turn to the right side, press lightly on the edges. Top-stitch all round, $\frac{1}{8}$in (3mm) from the edges.

13 Bound edging: To work this, place the wadding on the wrong side of the lining with the quilt front on top, face upwards. Smooth the quilt from the middle outwards and, as you smooth, pin round the edges. Baste and remove the pins. Trim the edges even.

14 Cut 3in (7.5cm)-wide strips of contrasting fabric on the straight grain, to fit the quilt sides, plus 1in (2.5cm) on each strip.

15 Fold the strips lengthways and press the crease. Press under $\frac{1}{2}$in (1cm) hems. Pin the strips to the quilt edges, right sides facing. Apply the two long sides first, then the short sides, overlapping the strips at the corners and turning in the ends neatly. Machine-stitch through all thicknesses.

Scale: 1 sq = 1in (2.5cm)

Butterfly

Crocodile

Ideas for patterns

The animals, flowers and bird shapes can be used for different decorative effects in a child's room. For instance, trace the shapes onto stencil blanks and decorate the walls with a frieze.

Traced down onto cotton fabrics, you might colour in the animals and bird with fabric paints, adding tendrils of vines between the creatures and putting in more leaves and butterflies, to make a jungle scene for a bed cover or a wall panel.

Use fabric painting for making nursery pictures also, or for book covers.

If the patterns were enlarged, attractive soft toys might be made. Draw the patterns on fabric twice, reversing one shape. Colour with fabric paints. Cut out with $\frac{1}{4}$in (6mm) seam allowance all round. Put two shapes together, right sides facing and stitch round, leaving a gap for turning. Turn right side out, stuff and close the seam.

Tiger

Swings mobile

Boys and girls come out to play under the tree on this innovative mobile. It is a simple and inexpensive toy to make, mostly using scraps of coloured paper and knitting wool.

Materials
Squared pattern paper
Thin cardboard for templates
9 × 10in (23 × 25cm) piece of stiff, thin cardboard
9 × 20in (23 × 50cm) piece of green felt
Small pieces of stiff paper, white, blue, yellow, red, peach and light brown
Brown and yellow knitting wool
Red and blue felt-tipped pens
Adhesive
1yd (1m) approximately ½in (1cm)-wide green satin ribbon
9 red beads, 9 green beads
Green pearl cotton
Wire paper clip

Preparation
1 Draw the patterns for the tree and dolls' tops on squared paper. Stick to thin card and cut out for templates.

2 For the tree, cut 2 shapes from cardboard and 4 from green felt.

3 For the boy dolls, cut 5 tops from white paper. Cut 5 blue paper strips each 1⅛in × 11in (3 × 28cm) for trousers.

4 For the girl dolls, cut 2 dresses from red paper and 2 dresses from yellow paper. Cut 2in (5cm) circles for under the dolls, 2 yellow and 2 red.

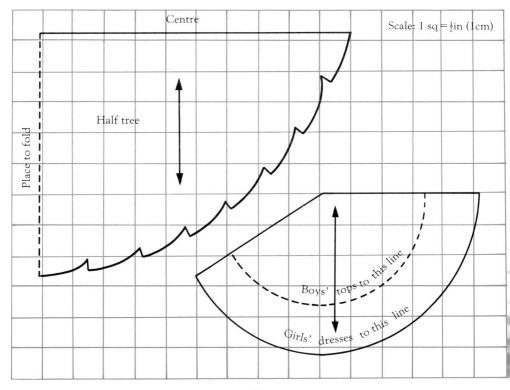

Centre

Scale: 1 sq = ½in (1cm)

Half tree

Place to fold

Boys' tops to this line

Girls' dresses to this line

54

5 For the heads, cut 9 strips of pink paper $\frac{3}{4} \times 6$in (18 mm × 15cm). For the arms cut 5 strips of white paper, 2 of red paper and 2 of yellow, each $3\frac{3}{8} \times \frac{1}{2}$in (8.5 × 1cm). Cut $\frac{1}{2}$in (1cm)-long pieces of pink paper for hands. Stick to the ends

of the arms and then round off the corners for hands. For the legs, cut 9 strips of pink paper $3\frac{3}{8} \times \frac{1}{2}$in (8.5 × 1cm).

6 Curl the garments pieces and heads by pulling them over a knife blade.

7 SWINGS: Cut 9 strips of cardboard, each 1 × 2¼in (2.5 × 6cm). Stick light brown paper to both sides to make the swings seats. For the swing ropes, cut 9 strips of light brown paper each ⅜ × 11in (9mm × 28cm).

Working the design
8 TREE: Stick the felt shapes to each side of the cardboard. Cut leaf-shaped holes at random in each 'branch'. Cut the curved edges into leaf shapes. To assemble the tree, cut a slot in both pieces, on one from the curved edge, and from the straight edge on the other. Push the two pieces together at right angles. Pierce holes at the intersection, using a thick needle. Pass a piece of stiff wire (such as a straightened paper clip) through the holes and twist the ends to hold the tree shape.

9 Cut several red paper apples, ½in (1cm) in diameter, and stick them to the tree.

10 GIRL DOLLS: Roll the dress into a cone shape and stick the straight edges together, overlapping them by ¼in (6mm).

11 HAIR: Roll the head strip into a tube about ¾in (18mm) diameter and stick over the dress cone point. To make the hair, wind wool 8 times round three fingers. Tie the loops together at the top, stick

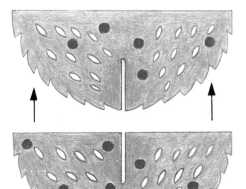

Fit the two tree pieces together on the slots.

the tie inside the top of the head. Stick loops to each side of the head. Draw on the features.

12 ARMS AND LEGS: Apply adhesive to the middle of the arms piece and stick over the join in the dress. Cut the legs strip into 2 pieces. Colour about ½in (1cm) of one end of each for shoes, then round off the corners. Stick the other ends under the dress hem so that about 1in (2.5cm) protrudes. Bend up the legs, and the shoes. Stick the under-dress circles of paper in place.

13 BOYS: Roll and stick the paper tops as for the girl's dresses. Roll the trouser strip into a 1in (2.5cm)-diameter tube and stick the overlap. Spread adhesive on the top edge and stick inside the cone top. Roll the head strip, secure and stick over the cone tip. Make hair by winding wool 4 times round two fingers and stick over the top of the head. Draw on the face. Fix the arms and legs in place, as for the girl dolls.

14 SWINGS: Stick the ends of the rope strip under the ends of the seat.

Finishing
15 Sew a ribbon loop to the top middle of the tree to hang the mobile. Holding each swing by the middle of the rope, balance a doll on the seat, then stick in place.

16 ASSEMBLY: Tie a green bead to the end of an 18in (45cm) length of thread. Pass the other end into a needle. Push the needle upwards through the middle of the swing rope, then through the tree centre and through a red bead. Tie the thread loosely, adjust the length to about 12in (30cm). This will be the longest thread of the mobile.

17 Fasten the other swings in the same way, varying the length of thread and adjusting the threads to balance the mobile. Secure thread ends with a dab of adhesive.

Fabric and ribbons basket

This woven basket is ideal for filling with small gifts for a new baby. Afterwards, it can be used in the nursery for creams, powders, tissues and wipes etc.

Materials
18 × 45in (45 × 115cm) piece of finely woven cotton fabric
18 × 45in (45 × 115cm) piece of thin wadding
5 × 31in (13 × 80cm) piece of white cotton
3yd (2.80cm) velvet ribbon, ¼in (6mm) wide
30in (75cm) of 1in (2.5cm)-wide broderie anglaise edging
7 × 21in (18 × 53cm) of heavyweight non-woven interfacing

Preparation
1 Cut a piece of printed fabric to 18 × 28in (45 × 70cm) and a piece of wadding to the same size. Baste them together on the edges.

2 To make the weaving strips for the basket sides, the fabric is stitched to the wadding, then cut into strips. Using a ruler and chalk (or a washable fabric pen), mark the fabric on the right side, starting ¼in (6mm) from one long edge. Mark off 2½in (6cm) sections with ½in (1cm) between each section.

3 Cut 2 circles of interfacing each 6¼in (16cm) diameter for the basket base. Baste them together on the edges. Cut another circle of interfacing for the lining, this time 5½in (13cm) diameter.

Working the design
4 On the marked, mounted fabric stitch along the marked lines. Cut the fabric into 6 strips along the centre of the ½in (1cm) spaces.

5 With the wadding on the inside, fold the strips lengthways, matching raw edges, then stitch again over the previous row of stitching. Bring the seam to the centre and press, very lightly, without flattening the wadding.

6 WEAVING THE BASKET: Work on an ironing board or a padded surface. Cut a piece of scrap fabric 5 × 2in (12.5 × 5cm). Baste, then stitch the end of each padded strip to this, spacing them so that together they measure 4½in (11cm) across. The seams should be face down. Pin the spare fabric down firmly.

7 Pin one end of the ribbon to the top of the right-hand strip and weave the end under and over the strips to the left. Bring the ribbon over the left-hand strip, twisting it to the right side and continue weaving to the right. The ribbons should lie about 1in (2.5cm) apart.

8 Continue weaving until the work measures about 21in (53cm) long. (You may have a surplus of the padded strips at the end.) Catch the ribbon end to the wrong side of the weaving.

9 ASSEMBLING THE BASKET: Baste, then stitch across the end of the weaving. Cut off the surplus within ¼in (6mm) of the weaving. Right sides facing, join the short ends. Turn to the right side. To attach the base, pin the 2 circles of interfacing, together, to the wrong side of the printed cotton fabric and cut out with 1in (2.5cm) all round. Pin the smaller interfacing circle to the white fabric, cut out with 1in (2.5cm) all round. Clip into the edges, turn the tabs to the wrong side and baste.

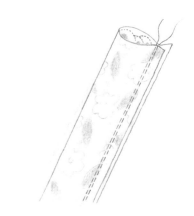

Wadding on the inside, match raw edges and stitch the strip again.

10 Pin the basket to the base and sew the base in place, working from the outside, and working the stitches through the ribbon only. Gather the broderie anglaise and fit it round the inside top of the basket. Slipstitch in place and oversew the cut ends.

11 HANDLE: From the remaining printed fabric, cut and make 3 more strips, as you did for the basket sides strips, each 18in (45cm) long. Plait the strips together tightly, baste, then stitch across the ends, trimming any surplus. Sew the ends to the inside top of the basket sides.

Baste and stitch the strips to the fabric scrap.

12 LINING: Cut a piece of lining fabric 5 × 21in (13 × 53cm). Right sides facing, join the short ends, turn to the right side. Press a ½in (1cm) hem to the wrong side on the top edge and gather, just under the folded edge. Gather within ½in (1cm) of the lower edge. Pull up the top gathering to fit inside the basket and then pull up the lower gathering. Place the lining in the basket and catch the upper edge over the broderie anglaise trimming and the handle ends.

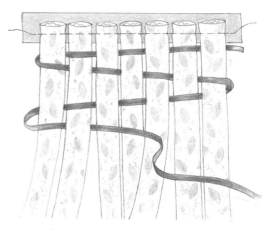

13 Insert the lining-covered interfacing circle. Remove all basting.

Starting at the right-hand side, weave under and over the strips to the left.

Keepsakes box

Most mothers treasure little mementoes of their babies. Decorate a special box with a painted design to keep the mementoes together. It makes a delightful new baby gift.

Trace, or use this graph pattern as required

Materials

Tracing or squared pattern paper
Wooden box with a top approximately
   7 × 10in (18 × 25cm), stripped and
   sanded smooth
Wood primer, fine sandpaper
Crafts paints; matt varnish

Preparation

1 Paint the box with primer. When dry,
smooth down with fine sandpaper.

2 The box pictured was painted first with
deep blue paint, then a coat of turquoise.
The final coat of turquoise was mixed
with a little white and a touch of black.
Paint was applied roughly so that
previous coats showed through a little.
Paint can be wiped from corners and
edges to give an 'antiqued' look. Paint the
inside edges of the box and lid.

Working the design

3 Trace the patterns on pattern paper.
(Alternatively, enlarge the graph pattern
as required.) Transfer the designs to the
box top and sides. Paint the design,
following the picture. Paint the central
oval white with a dark, outer shadow and
add the baby's initials.

4 Varnish the box all over.

Lining boxes

Measure the box sides, the lid and
the base. Draw the shapes onto thin
card. Draw a second line ¼in (6mm)
inside the outline. Place the card
pieces on medium-weight interfacing.
Trace round twice. Cut out, adding
¼in (6mm) all round. Stick the
interfacings to each side of the card
pieces, turning the edges in.
   Place the covered card pieces on
fabric. Trace round. Cut out, adding
¼in (6mm) all round. Place the fabric
on the right side of the covered
pieces, stick down the turnings on
the wrong side. Stick the lining
pieces to the inside of the box.

Teddy bear découpage jar

An ordinary jam or jelly jar can be transformed into a useful and attractive accessory with just cut-out paper motifs, adhesive and paint – plus, of course, a ribbon bow!

Materials
Glass jar (or other container)
Motifs for cutting out
PVA water-soluble adhesive
Modeller's paint
Ribbon trimming

Preparation
1 Wash the jar thoroughly making sure that any residue of label glue is removed. Dry and polish the jar with a warm dry cloth.

2 Using curved nail scissors, cut out motifs. Take great care at this stage because careful cutting out is the secret of good découpage. Hold the scissors so that the blades curve towards your body and cut with little 'feathering' movements so that the edge is slightly serrated. (This helps the paper to adhere more firmly when it is stuck down.)

Working the design
3 Spread adhesive very thinly on the front of the motif, right up to the edges. Position the motif on the inside of the jar, front side to the glass.

4 Smooth out any air bubbles with a finger tip. Make sure the motif is stuck down to the glass on all the edges. Remove any excess adhesive that seeps out with a dampened cotton wool bud. Leave to dry.

5 Use the paint fairly thick and only have a little on the brush tip. Dab paint over the inside of the glass, working very slowly and carefully. Use as little paint as possible for this first coat. Paint all over the back of the motif. Leave to dry.

6 Dab on a second coat if the découpage seems to need it. Finish the jar with a ribbon bow.

Dab paint carefully on the inside of the jar, covering the glass and the back of the motifs.

Ducks cross stitch picture

This charming nursery picture is so simple that it could be worked in an evening for a last-minute gift. The standing duck motif could also be embroidered on a bought feeder or a little dress.

Materials
Piece of white Aida fabric, 12 holes to 1in (2.5cm)
Stranded embroidery cottons, dark yellow, orange, mid-green, pale green, blue and black

Preparation
1 Mark the middle of the fabric with basting threads, horizontally and vertically. Count squares on the chart and mark the middle of it.

Working the design
2 Following the colour chart, work the design in cross stitches, using 2 strands of thread together, and starting in the middle of the chart.

3 Work the eyes in three-quarter cross stitches (or, if you prefer, work French knots using black cotton.

4 Press the finished embroidery on the wrong side. Mount the embroidery on a self-adhesive mounting board, and trim to size for framing.

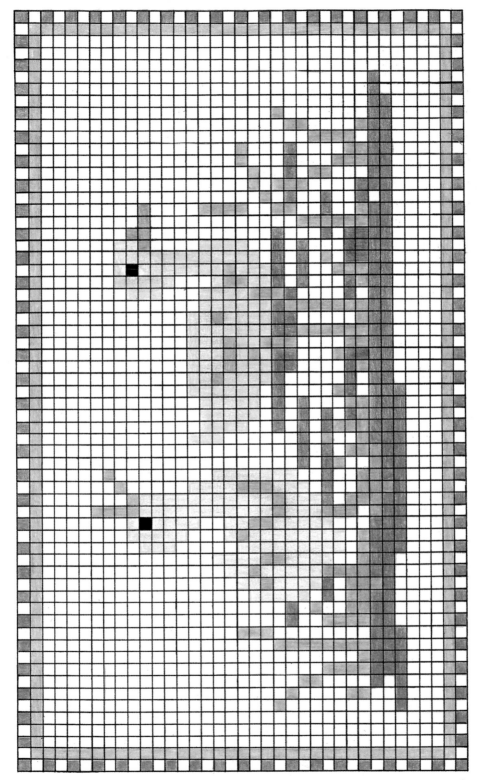

Cat tissue box cover

Pretty box covers are welcome gifts and this one makes an amusing addition to the nursery. The measurements are for a small rectangular box but you could adapt them to a larger box.

Materials
For a box approximately 5½ × 9 × 3in
  (13 × 23 × 7.5cm)
Tracing paper
21 × 15in (30 × 38cm) piece of patterned
  fabric
12 × 25in (30 × 65cm) piece of plain fabric
12 × 15in (30 × 38cm) piece of thin,
  polyester wadding
6 × 12in (15 × 30cm) piece of white fabric
  (pillow and sheet)
Small piece of fluffy, beige fabric
Small piece of fluffy, pink fabric
Scraps of felt, pink, dark grey
Stranded embroidery cottons
Washable polyester toy filling
6in (15cm) of narrow satin ribbon

Machine-stitch the diamond pattern and round
the box top. Cut away the corners.

Preparation
1 Lay the tissue box on tracing paper and draw round the outline. Fold the pattern twice to mark the middle of each side, then fold again to mark the sides into quarters. Cut out the pattern.

2 Pin the pattern to the middle of the right side of the printed fabric. Draw round the rectangle and mark in the quarters. Unpin the pattern and join the marks, thus making a diamond pattern.

3 Extend the outside lines of the pattern to the edges of the fabric (this will help in making up later).

4 Pin the pattern to the centre of the lining fabric, draw round and then extend the outside lines as you did for the patterned outer fabric. Cut away the corner areas (refer to the pattern).

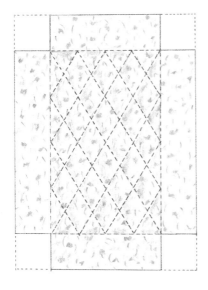

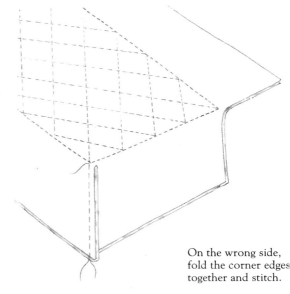

On the wrong side, fold the corner edges together and stitch.

Working the design

5 Baste the wadding and outer fabric together round the edges. Machine-quilt along the diamond pattern lines and round the outline of the box top. Cut away the fabric at the corners. Mark a 4in (10cm) line down the centre of the box top for the opening.

6 CORNERS: On the quilted outer, fold the edges of the cut-away corners together, right sides facing, and machine stitch. Work the corners of the lining in the same way. Slip the outer onto the lining and pin together. Mark a line 4in (10cm) long down the middle of the top. Using strips of the lining fabric, bind the edges (as you would when making a bound buttonhole). Put the cover on the box and pencil a line round, 1in (2.5cm) above the lower edge of the box. Trim away the fabric up to the line.

7 Cut the remaining lining fabric into 2¾in (7cm)-wide bias strips. Join strips to make a strip 42in (107cm) long. Fold the strip lengthways, gather up to fit round the box cover. Join the short ends. Baste to the right side of the quilted cover only, matching raw edges. Stitch, taking a ¼in (6mm) seam. Press the edges up on the wrong side of the cover. Fold in the lining edges and slipstitch to the quilted cover.

Cat and pillow

8 Trace the patterns for the head, paws and ears. Use the patterns to cut 2 front heads and 1 back head on the fold, 2 ears and 2 paws from the fluffy beige fabric. Cut 2 pink ears and 2 pink paws. (A seam allowance of ¼in (6mm) is included.)

9 Right sides facing, join the centre front head along A-B then join the front head to the back head (B-C, B-C). Turn the head right side out and stuff. Oversew the neck edges together. Make up 2 ears (pink lined) and 2 paws. Stuff the paws.

10 Oversew the bottom edges of the paws and ears. Embroider straight stitch

claws on the paws. Catch the ears to the head, pink side forwards. Cut a pink felt nose and sew it to the centre front seam of the head. Embroider a pink, smiling mouth in stem stitch and closed, grey eyes. Work the grey whiskers in straight stitches.

11 PILLOW AND SHEET: Cut a piece of white fabric 6in (15cm) square, fold it across, right sides facing and stitch round, leaving a gap. Turn right side out, stuff lightly and close the gap. Sew the cat head to the pillow along the side seams. Sew the paws either side of the head, just under the pillow edge.

12 Cut another 6in (15cm) of fabric, fold and stitch as before. Turn but do not stuff. Close the seam. Sew the bottom edge of the pillow to the sheet so that the paws lie on the sheet. Sew the sheet to the box top at one end. Tie a small ribbon bow and sew under the cat's chin.

Adapting the pattern

The little cat head could be adapted to other animals by using a different fabric colour, cutting suitable ears (long ears for a rabbit, round ears for a teddy bear). Or, a small doll's head could be made. Cut the head from pink or beige fabric and embroider closed eyes with eyelashes and a small smiling mouth. Sew doll's hair over the head or you could crochet curls directly onto the fabric.

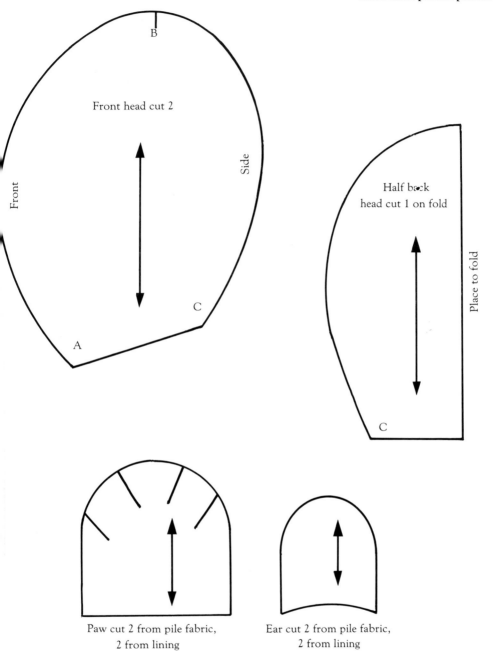

Front head cut 2

Front

Side

B

C

A

Half back
head cut 1 on fold

Place to fold

C

Paw cut 2 from pile fabric,
2 from lining

Ear cut 2 from pile fabric,
2 from lining

Baby slippers

These cosy little baby slippers would be welcomed by any mother. The slippers are sized for babies from 6 to 12 months old. Use soft, brushed cotton for the lining.

Materials
Squared pattern paper
28 × 12in (70 × 30cm) piece of outer
   fabric
Lining fabric to the same size
12in (30cm) of thin piping cord
12in (30cm) of 1in (2.5cm)-wide bias
   binding
12in (30cm) of ¼in (6mm)-wide elastic

Preparation
1 Draw the graph pattern on squared
paper (¼in (6mm) seam allowances are

included). Write in all the pattern marks.
Cut out the patterns. Cut out 2 soles, 2
uppers and 2 outers from both the outer
and lining fabrics.

Working the design
2 Baste bias binding round the cord, cut
the covered cord in two. Baste the
binding round the curved edges of the
upper, ½in (1cm) from the edge. Snip into
the seam allowance between A and B.

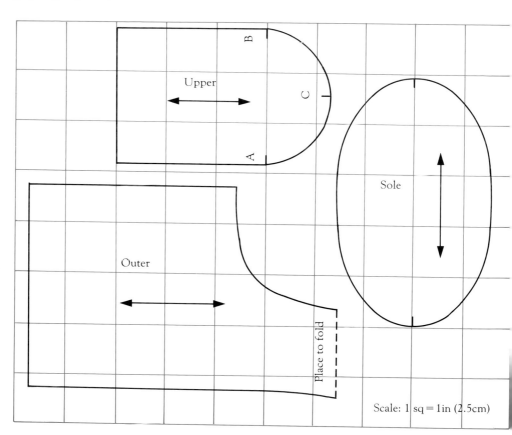

Scale: 1 sq = 1in (2.5cm)

3 Gather between A and B. Pin C on the upper piece to the centre front outer piece and match the top corners of the upper to the top corners of the outer piece. Baste and stitch, drawing up the gathering as necessary.

4 Open out the outer slipper; with wrong side facing you, pin one end of the elastic 1¾in (4cm) below the top straight edge at the centre back seam. Pin the other end at the corresponding spot,

stretching the elastic. Machine-stitch along the centre of the elastic. Join the centre back seam. Stitch the sole in place. Make up 2 outer slippers in the same way.

5 Make up the lining (but without elastic). Turn the outer slipper inside out and slip the lining onto it. Catch the soles together on the seam allowances. Turn in the top edge and slipstitch the lining to the outer.

Better Techniques

❧

In this chapter, you will learn the secrets of fine stencilling and wood painting, together with some tips on simple woodwork, plus hints for better sewing and embroidery.

STENCILLING

Stencilling is one of the simplest decorative techniques, and it is both inexpensive and stylish. It can be used in almost any room in the house, and on many kinds of plain wood furniture and wooden accessories.

In the nursery, stencilling really comes into its own and it is an ideal way of changing the decor as a baby grows into a toddler and then into a young child. Doors, walls, window surrounds – even bare floorboards – are areas where you might consider using stencilled effects. Cupboards, boxes, chests, shelves, lamp bases and table and chairs – all these can be colourfully decorated with motifs or borders. The sheep and shepherd motifs are trace-off patterns for you to try this craft. Trace and retrace the patterns as you require for a border or you can use the motifs singly, then prepare your stencil.

Basic equipment
Stencils
Although there are many ready-made, pre-cut stencils on the market there will be times when you want to cut your own. The best kind of stencil blank is made of transparent plastic film, matt on one side (for drawing the design) and shiny on the other.

Cutting mat
For ease of working, it is worth investing in a double-sided PVC cutting mat. These have the advantage that they 'heal up'

after cutting on them so their useful life is quite long. Alternatively, use a piece of hardboard.

Cutting knife
The best cutting tool is a small craft knife with a long, straight, pointed blade marked into sections. As the tool becomes less sharp, the top section can be snapped off with pliers, leaving the next section ready to use.

Stencil paints
The type of paint you use depends, to an extent, on the surface you are decorating. For paper, poster paints are adequate. On walls and painted wooden surfaces, casein emulsion paints give an enduring, washable result. Some stencil enthusiasts like to use car spray paints and you may want to experiment with these. They dry quickly and the colour range is extensive but it is important to keep the work area well ventilated and you should also wear a protective mask over your nose and mouth.

For beginners working with walls, doors or wooden items, specialist stencil paints are recommended. They dry quickly which minimizes accidental smearing, they mix together well and subtle shading effects can be achieved. A special range is also available for stencilling on fabric.

Stencil brushes
These come in several sizes and have a short, stubby head. Have two or three

Trace these pattern pieces

The outlines given here for a shepherd, sheep and grass tufts, are ideal for stencils. Trace the shapes and transfer onto stencil blanks. Use the design to decorate walls and furniture.

When you are stencilling the tufts of grass, use two or three different shades of green. Put the darker green tufts near to the bottom of your design with the lightest at the top.

73

sizes ready for your first project, a large brush for the main design areas, a smaller brush for the medium-sized areas and a finer brush for details.

Other equipment
You will also need tracing paper, masking tape, drawing pens, pencils, small foil containers, and a roll of kitchen paper. Protect your working surface with clean newspaper.

STENCILLING TECHNIQUES
Transferring the design
You can work in one of two ways. In the first, secure your drawn design to a cutting board with masking tape. Lay the clear plastic stencil blank on top, matt side up and tape it down. Using a drawing pen, trace the design onto the stencil blank.

In the second method, trace the design onto tracing paper. Spray the back with adhesive and place the design, face upwards, on the stencil blank.

Cutting the stencil
Hold the cutting tool like a pencil. In the beginning, you will find it helpful to stand and bend over your work while you are cutting. In this position it is easier to move your cutting arm from the shoulder and this helps you to cut more smoothly.

Insert the point of the blade slightly beyond the corner of a shape, then pull the knife towards you. Cut as far as you can in one movement then remove the tool. Begin cutting again, always drawing the blade towards you.

If you are cutting in a circle, leave the point of the blade in place and rotate the stencil with your left hand while you continue the cut. Remove cut sections as you work towards the edges of the design.

Stencil designs have 'bridges' between areas to separate colours and to retain the stencil's rigidity. If a bridge is accidentally cut and falls out it can be repaired with a tiny sliver of stencil blank stuck in place with colourless, all-

Trace the design onto the stencil blank.

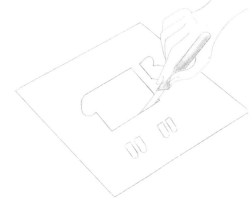

Cut the stencil, drawing the blade towards you.

Hold the brush like a pencil. Dab colour from the outer edges inwards.

purpose adhesive. After cutting the stencil, remove all the cut-away pieces.

Preparing to paint

Pour a little paint into a small receptacle – a foil container is ideal. Mix it with a thin wooden stick to an even consistency. Fold a few sheets of kitchen paper into a thick pad.

Applying the colours

It is important that the stencil is firmly attached to the surface and the best way to do this is to use a spray adhesive so that the stencil can be repositioned. Spray the reverse side of the stencil then press it onto the surface being decorated.

The stencil can also be secured with strips of masking tape, or, if just one small motif is being worked, you may be able to hold it in place with your fingers.

Dip the tip of the brush into paint then dab the brush up and down on the pad of kitchen paper until it is almost dry.

Hold the brush as you would a pen. Starting at the outer edges of the stencil and working in a circular motion, transfer colour to the surface with an up and down dabbing movement. Work towards the centre of the area. Leave the colour to dry a little before gently lifting off the stencil.

If you are working a single colour repeat, move the stencil and secure it as before and repeat the painting process.

If you are using several colours, let the first colour dry before over-stencilling. You will find it helpful to have a separate brush for each colour.

> Small cosmetic sponges, used in the same way as stencilling brushes, are ideal applicators for larger areas.

Edge stencilling

A different effect can be achieved by using an edge stencil. Trace a shape (such as one of the sheep in the pattern provided). Cut the shape from a stencil blank. Hold the cut-out shape against the surface to be decorated. Dip a small make-up sponge in the paint, dry off on kitchen paper. Dab paint all round the shape to produce a white 'negative' design on a coloured background.

REMOVING ADHESIVES

If you are doing craftwork, inevitably you will be using glues and adhesives of different kinds. And, almost as inevitably, some adhesive will get onto clothes or furnishings. Adhesive manufacturers are very good about helping with advice about solvents for their products. Some will even supply solvents direct if you write to them. In general, the first step in glue first aid is to scrape off any deposit and then proceed as follows:

Clear adhesive

On the skin, wash first, then remove any residue with nail varnish remover. On clothing and furnishings, hold a pad of absorbent rag on the underside, dab with non-oily nail varnish remover on the right side.

Epoxy adhesive:

Lighter fuel or cellulose thinners will remove adhesive from the hands. On fabrics, hold a rag pad under the glue stain, dab with cellulose thinners on the right side. On synthetic fibres, use lighter fuel.

Adhesive tape residue:

White spirit or cellulose thinners may do it. Or try nail varnish remover. Adhesives vary and you will have to experiment.

Latex adhesive:

Lift off as much as possible before the adhesive hardens. Keep the glue soft with cold water and rub with a cloth. Treat any stains with liquid dry cleaner. Scrape off any deposits with a pencil rubber.

WOODWORK
Tools and equipment
While it is possible to make simple things in wood using the minimum of tools, one or two mechanical aids will make your work easier.

Jig saw (fretsaw)
This tool is available with a variety of detachable blades, each for the type of wood you are cutting.

Finishing sander
A finishing sander will save you hours of work. They come with different grades of sand paper and a beautiful finish to work is easily achieved.

Jig saws (fretsaws) come with a variety of blades.

Try-square
This has a wooden or plastic stock and a metal blade at right angles. This essential piece of equipment is needed to ensure that all joints and edges are cut at right angles. It will also be used to check that pieces will fit well together.

Using a try-square Before starting any woodwork project you should mark the face side and the face edge of the wood. This is the surface that will show when the work is finished. When taking any check with the try-square, its wooden handle should always be laid against the face side of the wood.

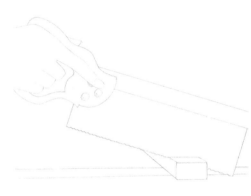
Working with a tenon saw.

Tenon saw
This is used for cutting wood and will probably be the most useful tool in your toolbox. It has a rigid blade with pointed teeth. Choose either a 10 or 12in (25 or 30cm) saw with 14 to 16 teeth.

Using a tenon saw When you are using a tenon saw for cutting wood, mark the cutting line on the face side of the wood, then lay the try-square along the face side to mark the cutting line, first on one edge and then on the other. Finally, mark the back of the wood and shade off the waste part which is to be cut away.

Cuts are always made on the waste side of the marked lines. This makes sure that the thickness of the saw will not cut away part of the shape you are making. Start

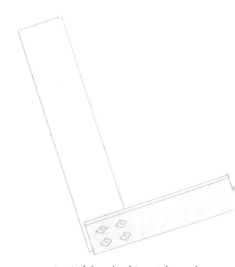
A try-square is vital for checking right-angles.

the cut by placing your left thumb against the saw blade and make a light cut to begin, then start sawing along the whole length of the saw blade. If the blade will not move smoothly try stroking a scrap of wax candle along the teeth. Keep the saw upright while working. When the end of the cut is reached saw very lightly to avoid the wood breaking off and splintering underneath. Then check against the marked lines to make sure that you have cut the wood at the right angles. The edge of the wood can be lightly planed if necessary so that the cut is where you intended.

Cordless screw driver

This is a great asset to a woodworker. It will drive screws into wood effortlessly and accurately.

Using the screwdriver Drill a shallow pilot hole which is the same diameter as the straight part of the screw (just beyond the head). This will make sure that the screw goes straight into the wood.

Work bench and clamp

A strong table or work bench is essential for wood work and, wherever possible, work should be clamped to the bench. Use a piece of scrap wood under the metal pad of the clamp so that it does not crush and mark the work.

Other items of equipment

To make simple toys and accessories, you will probably need the following items: a drill and bits, including countersinking bits, wood glue, glass and sandpaper in various grades, screws and nails and a hammer.

An extra fine finish can be given to wood if, when you have finished the final sanding, the work is wetted with clean water. Leave it to dry and the grain will have raised. A final sanding with a fine grade paper will give a silky smoothness, ideal for painting or varnishing.

Painting wood

Wood should be very smooth before painting and this may take several sandings, finishing with the very finest grade. Nails should be punched below the surface and any holes or blemishes filled with wood filler.

If you are making a toy, take great care that only non-toxic paint is used. Always take the advice of the supplier. Tiny tins of gloss or matt craft paints, available in a wide range of colours, are ideal for painting small toys. There is also a kind of craft paint that is diluted with water. This type of paint is used when you want the wood grain to show.

Getting a good finish

Getting a really good painted finish takes time and preparation. Prime the wood with primer, then apply two thin coats of a suitable undercoat. Diluted emulsion paint makes a good undercoat. Rub the dry undercoat smooth again if bits of paint have stuck to the surface.

Before applying the final gloss coat, choose a fairly warm day if possible and do not wear anything woolly! Close the windows if there is a breeze which might bring hairs and dust into contact with your work.

Dip the bristles of the brush into the paint and draw the brush against the side of the tin to remove excess paint and any drips. Apply the paint lightly and immediately begin to brush out. This means spreading the paint in all directions from where you applied it. You will be surprised how far one brush-load of paint will go! Try to achieve a really thin coat of paint over the surface. Finally, brush out with all the strokes going in one direction lifting the brush into the air at the end of a stroke. In a few minutes, the surface will have smoothed itself out. Leave to dry, under cover if possible.

SEWING AND EMBROIDERY

A knowledge of needlecrafts is useful if you are making soft toys and furnishings. Here are some of the techniques you will find useful.

Appliqué

This is term given to the technique of applying pieces of fabric to a ground fabric decoratively. Appliqué can be worked by machine, using straight stitch, zigzag stitch or satin stitch. The edges of the appliqué fabric can be worked raw or turned under. When the fabric edges are turned, hand sewing is generally used to attach the piece, either hemming or slip stitching. Decorative embroidery stitches are also used in some types of appliqué.

Detached appliqué This seems a contradiction in terms but all it means is that a decorative piece is made up separately, sometimes stuffed or interfaced, and is then attached to the background fabric. The piece may be permanently attached with sewing, sometimes leaving the edges free, or it may be made to be removable, fixed in place temporarily with press fasteners or touch-and-hold fastening.

TOUCH-AND-HOLD FASTENING

This is a tape made of nylon and consists of two strips, one with a hooked nap and the other with a looped nap. When pressed together these intermesh and hold the two sides together. The tape is easily pulled apart to unlock.

To apply the tape, position and baste the hooked side on the underlap. Stitch round through all layers. Position and baste the looped side on the overlap. Stitch round through all layers.

TOP-STITCHING

Top-stitching is done from the right side of the piece. Set the sewing machine to a medium-to-large stitch and stitch between $\frac{1}{8}$–$\frac{1}{4}$in (3–6mm) from the finished edge. Use ordinary sewing thread or a silk twist.

STITCHES

The term 'stitching' usually means working on a sewing machine, using either straight stitch or zigzag stitch. The term 'sewing' means working by hand. Seams can be worked by hand using running stitches or back stitching. You will also use oversewing to neaten edges and slipstitching to close gaps in seams.

Oversewing

Working from right to left, bring the needle through at A and insert it from the back of the work at B, bringing it through to the front at C, ready to start the next stitch.

Oversewing.

Slipstitching

Work from right to left and bring the needle up through the folded edge of the fabric. Pick up a thread or two on the opposite edge then slip the needle through the folded edge for about $\frac{1}{8}$in (3mm). Bring the needle through and pull gently.

Slipstitching.

Sewing with felt

Cut felt shapes in the same way as woven fabric, pinning the pattern to the felt. When cutting out small shapes, either iron the felt onto interfacing to stiffen the edges, or press the felt onto a small self-adhesive label. This helps you to cut out with a firm edge. Felt can be machine-stitched or hand-sewn with running stitches. Use machine-zigzag for neatening edges.

EMBROIDERY STITCHES

French knot

Bring the needle through at A, wind the thread round the needle twice and then insert the point at B, close by A. Pull the thread through so that the knot tightens on the surface.

French knot.

Chain stitch

Bring the needle through at A and, with the thread below the needle, insert it beside A at B. The thread forms a loop. Bring the needle through at C, pull through gently, ready to start the next chain stitch.

Chain stitch.

Fly stitch

Bring the needle through to the front of work at A, insert it at B and bring it out again at C. Work a small couching stitch over the loop to hold the fly stitch.

Fly stitch.

Back stitch

This stitch, properly worked, looks like machine-stitching and can be used for seaming. Come through at A, insert at B, come through at C.

FASTENINGS

If you are making clothes or furnishings for small children, the fastening method you choose is important. Press fasteners are very popular because they are easy for children to cope with and buttonholes tend to wear out. It is a good idea to use press fasteners and then sew a button on the outside of the garment for decoration.

Hooks and eyes are rather fiddly for children's hands. Zip fasteners are good, especially if they have large toggles.

Fabric or ribbon ties are ideal for babies clothes. To attach these, fold over one cut end and sew to the garment with tiny hemming stitches. Cut the other end of the tie in a fishtail or neaten it by turning a narrow doubled hem and hemming.

Ribbons or tapes through stitched casings are a pretty way of gathering necklines, cuffs and waists of children's clothes. To make a casing on an edge, turn and press a narrow hem, then turn the hem again to the desired depth. Machine-stitch along the top fold and then along the bottom fold.

Snip a hole in the casing in an unobtrusive place and oversew the edges to prevent them from fraying. Thread ribbon or tape (or elastic) through the casing using a bodkin.

For a young child, it is a good idea to pull the ribbon up to the desired fullness then catch it in place with a few stitches so that the ribbon cannot be pulled from the casing.

Buttons

Buttons must always be firmly sewn on. Thread the needle with strong thread and knot the end. Bring the needle through in the position of the button. Pass the needle up through one of the button holes and down through the other. Continue in the same way until the holes are filled with thread. If the button has four holes, work two opposite holes first, then the two remaining holes, forming a cross of stitches.

Imperial and metric measurements
Both imperial and metric
measurements are given in this book.
Choose either system to work to but
do not attempt to use both, nor try
and convert a measurement.
Measurements have been rounded
off for ease of working, unless the
measurement is critical, when an
exact conversion has been provided.